GW01159282

Original title:
Blueprint of Dreams

Author: Tim Wood
ISBN HARDBACK: 978-9916-88-046-3
ISBN PAPERBACK: 978-9916-88-047-0

Inked Reveries on Canvas

In whispers soft, the colors play,
Dreams entwined in hues of gray.
Each stroke a thought, a fleeting wish,
Captured in art, life's tender dish.

The palette speaks of joy and pain,
Memories linger, like gentle rain.
A canvas bare, now filled with light,
Inked reveries take their flight.

Constructing a Dreamscape

Brick by brick, the visions form,
In twilight's glow, they break the norm.
A staircase leads to realms unknown,
Where every thought is overthrown.

Gardens bloom in colors bright,
Whispers echo through the night.
Building castles in the air,
In this dreamscape, free from care.

The Design of Infinite Possibilities

In every line, a tale unfolds,
A map of dreams, where hearts are bold.
Blueprints drawn with hope and grace,
A journey crafted, find your place.

With every step, new paths arise,
Underneath the boundless skies.
The design transcends the day,
Infinite possibilities guide the way.

Mapped in the Stars Above

Stars align in patterns bright,
Stories written in silver light.
Each constellation, a dream revealed,
Hope and wonder, forever sealed.

In twilight's gaze, we stand in awe,
Nature's canvas, without flaw.
Mapped in the stars, our fate displayed,
Eternal visions never fade.

Envelopes of Essence

In shadows soft, the whispers rise,
Wrapped in dreams where silence lies.
Each heartbeat echoes, pure and true,
Enveloped deep, the essence of you.

A gentle touch, the world we weave,
In corners where we dare believe.
Crafting moments, serene and bright,
In the envelopes of tender light.

Fractals of the Future

Patterns bloom in endless dance,
Mirrored stories, a second chance.
In the chaos, there's a plan,
Fractals unfold, the paths we span.

Infinite routes, forever bound,
In every echo, wisdom found.
Curved dimensions, time expands,
Fractals weave through shifting sands.

Audacity of Imagination

Beyond the stars, our thoughts take flight,
Boldly dreaming, igniting night.
With colors bright, we paint the skies,
In audacity, our spirit flies.

Chasing visions that dare to grow,
In realms where only hope can glow.
We carve our truths, defy the norm,
In imagination, we find our form.

Celestial Cartography

Maps of night, where starlight gleams,
Tracing paths of our brightest dreams.
Orbits dance in cosmic grace,
A celestial chart, our sacred space.

Through darkened skies, our guides align,
Constellations, stories intertwine.
In every spark, a universe flows,
Celestial maps, where wonder grows.

Scenarios of Serenity

In the hush of dawn, soft light unfolds,
Whispers of peace, a story retold.
Waves of tranquility kiss the shore,
Hearts ease their burdens, longing no more.

Among the trees, where shadows play,
Nature's embrace, a gentle ballet.
Birds sing sweetly, melodies soar,
In this calm space, we're free to explore.

Tides of Transformation

Beneath the moon's gaze, the ocean sighs,
   Ebb and flow, where the essence lies.
   Each wave a lesson, a tale of change,
   Shaping the shores, vast and strange.

Footprints washed away, yet still we tread,
In currents of time, where futures are bred.
  With each crashing wave, we start anew,
Tides of transformation, guiding us through.

Pathways to Possibility

A winding road, where dreams may bloom,
Paths intertwined, dispelling the gloom.
Every step taken, choices we make,
Carving our journey, the risks we stake.

Beneath the arching boughs, hope ignites,
Stars align softly, lighting the nights.
With open hearts, we dare to see,
Endless horizons, where we can be free.

The Architecture of Yearning

In the heart's quiet chambers, desires linger,
Blueprints of dreams crafted by tender fingers.
Wishes take shape like castles in the air,
Fragile yet sturdy, built from despair.

Through windows of longing, visions unfold,
Stories of passion, both vibrant and bold.
Each beam of hope, a testament true,
The architecture of yearning, ever in view.

Threads of a Visionary Tapestry

In the loom of dreams we weave,
Colors bright, we do believe.
Whispers dance on fabric's edge,
Stories told, a silent pledge.

Fingers trace the vibrant strands,
Crafting visions with gentle hands.
A tapestry that sings and glows,
Reflecting life's eternal flows.

Chasing Celestial Schematics

Stars aligned, a blueprint's call,
Mapping dreams where shadows fall.
Galaxies swirl in cosmic might,
Chasing wonders, the depths of night.

Nebulae glow with secrets bright,
Crafting worlds with pure delight.
Each twinkling star, a path to find,
Uniting hearts and cosmic mind.

Labyrinths of the Mind's Eye

Winding paths through thoughts so deep,
Echoes linger, secrets keep.
Mirrors crack, reflections flee,
Truths emerge from shadows, free.

In mazes built of dreams and fears,
We navigate through hopes and tears.
Unlock the doors, let visions rise,
Illuminating the darkest skies.

Patterns of Hope and Horizon

On the brink of dawn we stand,
Sketching futures in the sand.
Horizons whisper to our heart,
Every ending plays its part.

With each wave, the canvas swells,
Patterns emerge, bright tales to tell.
In the light of day, we find,
Hope entwined with every kind.

Landscapes of Laughter

In fields of joy where giggles roam,
The sun lays down a golden dome.
Children dance in playful cheer,
Echoing laughter we hold dear.

Beneath the trees, we find our space,
Sharing secrets, hearts embrace.
The brook hums sweet, a playful tune,
Nature's laughter in full bloom.

Canvases of Courage

Brush strokes bold on canvas bright,
Colors clash, defying night.
Each mark tells stories yet untold,
In every hue, a heart so bold.

With every challenge, brush we raise,
Creating futures in vibrant ways.
Courage whispers through the paint,
A symphony of dreams, no restraint.

Waves of Whimsy

The ocean laughs with gentle sway,
Tickling toes at the break of day.
Seashell secrets on the shore,
Whispers echo of what's in store.

Breezes dance with a playful kiss,
In every wave, a moment of bliss.
Chasing dreams on sandy trails,
Life's sweet journey never pales.

Dialogues of Dreams

In twilight's glow, the stars align,
We speak in whispers, soft and fine.
Each dream a thread, a mystic weave,
In shared hopes, we dare believe.

Through silken nights and dawn's embrace,
We journey forth, a fearless race.
With every word, we chart the skies,
In dialogues where futures rise.

Sketches of the Sublime

In dawn's embrace, the light unfolds,
Nature whispers, secrets untold.
Mountains stand, their majesty clear,
Hearts awaken, yearn, and cheer.

Clouds drift softly, like dreams in flight,
Colors blend at the edge of night.
Stars emerge, a glittering guide,
In silence, our souls reside.

Weavings of Wonder

Threads of gold and silver spun,
In the tapestry, life's stories run.
Moments captured, woven tight,
In the fabric, shadows and light.

Echoes linger in the air,
Laughter dances, a joyful prayer.
Each stitch a memory to hold,
In warmth, our lives are told.

Frameworks of Freedom

Under the sky, dreams take flight,
Boundless hopes soar into the night.
Chains of doubt, we break away,
With every step, we find our way.

Voices rise, a song of grace,
Together we build a safer place.
In unity, our spirits gleam,
In freedom, we dare to dream.

The Alchemy of Aspirations

Within the heart, a spark ignites,
Turning wishes into sights.
From lead to gold, we make our claim,
In the journey, we ignite the flame.

Visions swirl, a dance of fate,
Crafting futures, we create.
Through the fire, our dreams transpire,
In every heart, we lift desire.

Schemes of the Heart's Desire

In whispers soft, the longing grows,
A dance of hopes where rivers flow.
Each heartbeat dreams, a tale retold,
As love's bright fire warms the cold.

Beneath the stars, a wish takes flight,
To reach the dawn from endless night.
With every sigh, a spark ignites,
The schemes of hearts in silent nights.

Fragments of a Dreamer's Palette

Colors blend on a canvas wide,
Brushstrokes bold, where dreams reside.
Each hue a whisper, soft yet clear,
In realms of vision, far and near.

Dabs of hope, splashes of chance,
In every shade, a fleeting dance.
Fragments painted from soul's desire,
A palette rich, alive with fire.

Casting Shadows of Aspirations

In twilight dusk, ambitions soar,
Casting shadows to distant shore.
Each step a footprint on the sand,
A journey mapped by a steady hand.

With dreams that shimmer, shadows grow,
Paths illuminated by inner glow.
Aspiration's call, a beacon bright,
Guides the heart toward the light.

Cartography of a Fevered Imagination

Maps unfold in a fevered mind,
Journeys charted, the lost to find.
Each line a pulse, a heartbeat's trace,
In wild terrains of time and space.

Scribbled notes on the edges frayed,
In every sketch, a story played.
Imagination wanders without end,
In cartography where dreams transcend.

Blueprinted Visions in Twilight

In twilight's soft embrace we dream,
Lines drawn in whispers, shadows gleam.
Blueprints of thoughts take gentle flight,
Mapping the stars in fading light.

Each stroke a wish upon the night,
Crafted with hope, love's purest sight.
A canvas wide, where visions play,
Drawing the dawn from the end of day.

Imaginary Frameworks of Flight

Beneath the clouds, we weave our tales,
With soaring dreams, like wind in sails.
Frames of freedom in a vibrant sky,
Imagined wings that learn to fly.

Each thought takes off, a gentle breeze,
A dance of hope among the trees.
In sketches bold, we chase the dawn,
Through realms of dreams, where fears are gone.

Beyond the Horizon's Edge

Past the horizon, where colors blend,
Lies a pathway that has no end.
Curves of the earth wrap 'round the sun,
Chasing shadows till day is done.

Footsteps echo on the shore,
Waves of whispers, calling for more.
Adventurers brave, we seek the light,
Beyond the horizon, out of sight.

The Geometry of Wishful Thinking

In angles sharp, our dreams align,
Crafting shapes where stars entwine.
Theorems of hope in every thought,
Mapping the joys that life has sought.

With circles wide, our hearts expand,
In the geometry of a loving hand.
Equations of time, forever true,
In wishful thinking, we start anew.

Tapestry of Hope

Threads of light weave through the dark,
Stitching dreams into a vibrant spark.
Each moment a knot, each breath a thread,
In the tapestry of hope, we are led.

Silent whispers dance on the loom,
Creating a pattern that banishes gloom.
In every color, a story unfolds,
A tapestry of hope that never grows old.

With every stitch, we mend the fray,
Embracing the dawn of a brand new day.
Woven together, hearts intertwine,
In this tapestry, our spirits align.

Mosaics of Tomorrow

Shattered pieces lie on the ground,
From these fragments, beauty is found.
Each shard a vision, bright and clear,
In mosaics of tomorrow, we persevere.

Colors shift in the morning light,
Together we rise, banishing night.
Every tile a dream, bold and bright,
Crafting our future, igniting the fight.

The art of the past guides our way,
Forming a path where hopes can play.
In every reflection, a promise glows,
Mosaics of tomorrow, where courage grows.

Pillars of Imagination

Strong and steadfast, they reach for the sky,
Pillars of dreams, where thoughts can fly.
Each idea a beam, supporting the weight,
Building a world where we create our fate.

Imagination soars on wings of thought,
In this sacred space, wonders are sought.
Every whisper a brick, laid with care,
Pillars of imagination rise everywhere.

From the ground to the stars, they stretch wide,
Embracing the visions we hold inside.
In this realm, anything is possible and real,
Pillars of imagination, we joyfully feel.

Fragments of Fantasies

Scattered dreams like leaves in the breeze,
Whispering secrets with effortless ease.
Each fragment glimmers, a tale to share,
In the world of fantasies, beyond compare.

Through the shadows, they twirl and dance,
Inviting us into a beautiful trance.
In every glint, a spark of delight,
Fragments of fantasies igniting the night.

As we gather them close with gentle hands,
We weave them together in far-off lands.
In this mosaic, our hearts will sing,
Fragments of fantasies, our souls take wing.

Sketching the Sublime

In whispers soft, the clouds unfold,
A canvas bright, with dreams retold.
The sun dips low, a golden haze,
In twilight's grip, the heart's ablaze.

Brush strokes dance on twilight's seam,
Each hue a note, a silent dream.
Nature's breath, a stroke divine,
In every pulse, the stars align.

Patterns of Possibility

Beneath the stars, new paths we trace,
In shadows cast, we find our place.
Each choice a thread, a woven fate,
In life's vast loom, we contemplate.

Curves and lines, a world unfolds,
In whispered hopes, the future holds.
With every turn, the heart ignites,
In patterns drawn, our spirits rise.

Foundations of Wishfulness

Upon the ground where dreams take flight,
A soil rich with shared delight.
With roots that delve into the past,
We build our hopes, so strong, so vast.

In gentle hands, our wishes grow,
Awakening sparks in the flow.
The heart lays bricks, a structure bright,
In visions clear, we find our light.

Cartography of the Mind

In thought's expanse, we chart the way,
Through labyrinths where shadows play.
Each memory, a place we roam,
Mapping landscapes that feel like home.

The peaks of joy, the valleys deep,
In silent whispers, secrets keep.
With compass true, we navigate,
In the mind's eye, we create our fate.

Currents of Creation

In the heart of the silence, whispers arise,
Colors dance freely beneath the vast skies.
Threads of existence weave in the air,
Each moment a canvas, intricate and rare.

Rivers of thought in a flowing embrace,
Crafting our dreams in this timeless space.
Stars play their notes in a cosmic song,
Binding us gently, where we all belong.

With every heartbeat, the world spins anew,
Life finds its rhythm in shades of the blue.
Nature's own brush paints the landscape around,
In the depths of creation, true magic is found.

Awake to the wonders, let your soul soar,
Through currents of creation, seek evermore.
In the dance of existence, feel the divine,
For in every moment, our spirits entwine.

A Symphony in Blue

Gentle waves whisper on shores of the night,
Moonlight reflecting, the world clothed in white.
Notes of the ocean, a soft lullaby,
Echoes of dreams as clouds drift on high.

A canvas of azure, the horizon expands,
Where music and colors flow into our hands.
Every soft breeze brings a story to tell,
In the symphony of blue, our hearts break the shell.

Dancing with shadows that flicker and gleam,
In the twilight's embrace, we find our own dream.
Harmony whispered, the stars start to hum,
Guiding our spirits to places we come.

Night deepens softly, as silence holds sway,
With every heartbeat, the night gives way.
For in this grand symphony, we're never alone,
Each note that we play, together, our home.

Maps to the Heart's Desire

In shadows deep, we find our trace,
With every path, a soft embrace.
The winding roads, they lead us on,
To places where our dreams are drawn.

Through valleys low and mountains high,
The compass spins, we learn to fly.
Each turn a whisper, sweet and clear,
Guiding us toward what we hold dear.

In every step, a story told,
Of love and loss, of fierce and bold.
The map unfolds, as hearts conspire,
Leading us to our heart's desire.

So trust the roads that lie ahead,
For every tear, a joy instead.
With every journey, we will find,
The treasures deep within the mind.

Canvas of Tomorrow

Brush strokes dance on azure skies,
Colors bloom, our spirit flies.
In dreams we paint, the future bright,
With every hue, we chase the light.

Bold splashes speak of hopes anew,
As visions form, and passions brew.
Each canvas holds a promise near,
Of worlds unseen and paths sincere.

In strokes of gold and shades of gray,
We carve our fate, we find our way.
With every layer, dreams ignite,
On canvases of pure delight.

So wield the brush, let heart unfold,
Create the tales yet left untold.
With every vision, we will soar,
Painting life forevermore.

Echoes of Aspirations

In valleys wide, our hopes resound,
The echoes rise, they know no bounds.
Each whispered dream with fervor grows,
A symphony of heartbeats flows.

Through whispered winds and silent nights,
Our aspirations take to flights.
The stars above, they watch in awe,
As we pursue our deepest law.

In every challenge, echoes call,
A vibrant sound, that we stand tall.
With every step, the future sings,
A melody of splendid things.

So let the echoes guide us true,
With every breath, we start anew.
In unity, our voices blend,
A chorus strong that will not end.

Designs of the Soul

Intricate threads weave tales untold,
With patterns rich, in shades of gold.
Each design maps the heart's embrace,
In silences where thoughts find grace.

The fabric soft, yet oh so bright,
Reflects our dreams, our inner light.
In every stitch, a story sewn,
Of journeys made, and seeds we've grown.

Through winding lines, the spirit flows,
In every curve, our essence shows.
With designs crafted by the heart,
We find the place where we can start.

So cherish each and every thread,
For in the weave, our lives are read.
The fabric of the soul will play,
A symphony in bright array.

Horizons of the Heart

In twilight's glow, dreams take flight,
Where stars softly whisper through the night.
Each heartbeat sketches, a tale untold,
A canvas of wishes, bright and bold.

The sky's embrace, a gentle kiss,
As hearts collide in a dance of bliss.
Together we wander, hand in hand,
Chasing horizons, across the land.

With every wave that meets the shore,
Love blooms anew, forevermore.
In every sunrise, hope ignites,
Horizons beckon, pure delights.

Though shadows may linger, and storms may bide,
In the heart's expanse, we shall confide.
For love's horizon will always be,
The brightest path, in you and me.

Drafts of Destiny

In every breath, a choice unfolds,
Drafts of destiny written in gold.
A path uncharted, yet beckons near,
With every moment, the future's clear.

We sketch our dreams on paper fine,
With ink of hope, and love's design.
As visions merge, and time aligns,
In the fabric of fate, our heart entwines.

Through twists and turns, we learn to soar,
Drafting our lives, always wanting more.
With laughter lingering in the air,
Destiny whispers, a sweet affair.

So let us venture, hand in hand,
In this tapestry, so grand.
For every draft can lead to light,
In the dance of fate, we take our flight.

Weaving Whispers

In quiet corners, whispers flow,
Threads of secrets, gentle and slow.
We weave together, stories blend,
A tapestry rich, where dreams extend.

With every stitch, a bond is made,
In silken shadows, fears do fade.
A whispered promise, soft as lace,
In the loom of time, we find our place.

Through tangled paths, we learn and grow,
In whispered wishes, love's gentle glow.
Each moment captured, a precious art,
Weaving together, soul to heart.

So let us listen, to the winds that sigh,
In every whisper, love will lie.
For in this dance, we find our way,
Creating a world where hearts can stay.

Designs for the Deep

Beneath the waves, where dreams reside,
Lie secrets hidden, where fish abide.
With strokes of courage, we dive so steep,
To uncover wonders, plans we keep.

Inkelp forests sway with silent grace,
Creatures murmuring in a hallowed space.
Designs for the deep, a realm so vast,
We chart our course, as we swim past.

For every coral, a story's spun,
In shimmering light, our hearts are won.
With every ripple, we hear the call,
To explore the depths, where spirits enthrall.

So let us venture through waters blue,
In designs for the deep, we start anew.
With every heartbeat, our journey flows,
In the ocean's embrace, true love grows.

Choreography of Courage

In shadows deep, we find our way,
With every step, we choose to stay.
Through trials faced, our spirits rise,
In the dance of life, we claim the prize.

Brave hearts move with silent grace,
Defying fears, we embrace the space.
With every leap, the world appears,
Crafting strength from whispered fears.

The rhythm beats in unison,
As one, we rise, no longer lone.
Together we weave a brilliant thread,
In courage found, our lives are led.

In this ballet where hope ignites,
We write our fate in daring flights.
Each moment bold, we choose to soar,
A choreography forevermore.

The Fabric of Desire

Threads of passion weave through night,
In every glance, a spark ignites.
With hands entwined, we dare to dream,
In the fabric, love's gentle seam.

Colors blend in vibrant hues,
With whispered words, we craft our muse.
In tangled waves, our hearts align,
We stitch together, yours and mine.

A tapestry rich with fervent fire,
Each pattern tells a tale of desire.
In quiet moments, we breathe and find,
The beauty lies intertwined.

As daylight fades, our passion glows,
In every thread, the story flows.
Together we weave, endlessly spun,
The fabric of desire, two become one.

Framework of the Future

In dreams we build, with hands so strong,
The future calls us to belong.
Each foundation laid, a step in time,
A vision crafted, bold and prime.

With every doubt, we shape our fate,
A canvas waits, we hesitate.
Yet with each brush, the doubts unwind,
A masterpiece of heart and mind.

We rise like towers, reaching high,
Constructing hopes against the sky.
With courage as our guiding light,
The framework gleams through darkest night.

In unity, we forge ahead,
A legacy of dreams widespread.
With every heartbeat, love will steer,
In the framework of the future, we persevere.

Portraits of Potential

In every soul, a story hides,
With dreams entwined, our spirit rides.
A canvas blank, yet rich with grace,
Portraits of potential, time won't erase.

With gentle strokes, we paint our way,
Each hue a chance, a bright display.
In colors mixed, the shadows blend,
The light of hope, we will defend.

Through trials faced, we come alive,
In every struggle, we learn to thrive.
With open hearts, we share the view,
Potential shines, forever true.

In the gallery of what's to come,
We boldly stand, together, as one.
With every brush, our spirits soar,
In portraits crafted, forevermore.

The Palette of Promise

Colors swirl, the dawn's first light,
Whispers of hope take graceful flight.
Mixing dreams in every hue,
A canvas bright, a life anew.

Brushstrokes soft, yet bold and free,
Each stroke a chance, a destiny.
Crafting visions, hearts ignite,
In this art, we find our might.

Shadows fade, the night moves on,
Every challenge met at dawn.
With colors fierce, we paint the sky,
As promises flow, and doubts pass by.

In every shade, a tale unfolds,
A vibrant world that love beholds.
So take the brush, let spirits sing,
For in this palette, hope takes wing.

Constructs of Courage

Brick by brick, we build our dreams,
Foundations strong, or so it seems.
In the face of trials, we stand tall,
Constructing courage through it all.

Steel and stone, our hearts align,
With every challenge, we redefine.
Walls may crumble, yet we'll repair,
Generations built from love and care.

Ladders rise to heights unknown,
Overcoming fears, we've brightly grown.
With each step taken, we declare,
Courage thrives when hearts are bare.

In this fortress, we unite,
Fighting shadows, chasing light.
Hand in hand, we'll forge ahead,
With constructs strong, no words unsaid.

Spectrums of Surrender

In quiet moments, hearts unwind,
Releasing burdens, peace we find.
The colors shift, the skies transform,
In surrender's grace, we're reborn.

Waves of calm, the ebb and flow,
Letting go of what we know.
In vulnerability, we unite,
Embracing shadows, facing light.

Every tear, a seed of growth,
In surrender, we honor both.
Life's great spectrum, wide and free,
In allowing, we truly see.

So breathe the air, let worries fade,
In surrender's hands, we're not afraid.
The palette shifts, a dance so grand,
In every heartbeat, hope will stand.

Dreamscapes Unfurled

In whispered dreams, the night reveals,
A tapestry of light that feels.
Colors blend in twilight's embrace,
Through vivid realms, we find our place.

Stars ignite in endless skies,
Crafting worlds where magic lies.
In the silence, visions swirl,
Unlocking dreams, horizons twirl.

Pathways open, echoes call,
Through dreamscapes vast, we rise and fall.
With every heartbeat, visions soar,
In this canvas, we explore.

Awake or sleep, we dance with fate,
In dreams, we cherish, never wait.
With every spark, our spirits twirl,
In the dreamscapes, life unfurls.

Threads of Vision

In the fabric of dreams we weave,
Colors blend, and shadows cleave.
Whispers float on silken strands,
Guiding hearts with gentle hands.

Moments stitched beneath the moon,
Sewn with hope, before the dawn.
Each vision, a delicate thread,
Linking stories, softly spread.

The tapestry of time unfolds,
Secrets waiting to be told.
Artistry in light and dark,
Illuminating every spark.

In the loom of life, we find,
Threads that bind both heart and mind.
Woven stories, rich and true,
Threads of vision, me and you.

Imagery of the Infinite

Stars that dance in velvet skies,
Mirrored pools where silence lies.
Infinite dreams begin to flow,
Each moment, a chance to grow.

Waves of thoughts like oceans sweep,
Deepest whispers, secrets keep.
Colors swirl in cosmic flight,
Imagery of endless night.

Each heartbeat echoes through the void,
Time and space deftly employed.
Visions of eternity's grace,
Infinite journeys we embrace.

A canvas stretched beyond our sight,
Brushstrokes blending dark and light.
In the vastness, we discover,
Imagery painted, one another.

Castles in the Air

High above in azure blue,
Castles rise where dreams come true.
Turrets gleam in golden sun,
Imagined worlds where we have spun.

Bridges built of hope and fire,
Carried forth on wings of desire.
Here, the heart finds space to soar,
Castles in the air, evermore.

Clouds become our stepping stones,
Whispered hearts and softened tones.
In the heights, we learn to dare,
To build our dreams with love and care.

Fiction thrives where shadows play,
In the twilight, night meets day.
From these heights, we call and share,
With joy, we dwell in castles rare.

Lattice of Longing

Fractals intertwine and bend,
A lattice where all dreams extend.
Yearning hearts in patterns dance,
Lost in the depth of a fleeting glance.

Each thread a hope, each knot a chance,
Caught in the rhythm of circumstance.
Longing flows like river streams,
In a world that sighs and beams.

Beneath the lattice, shadows dwell,
Stories woven, rise and swell.
Silent wishes brush our skin,
As the tide of longing draws us in.

In the patterns, we find our way,
Mapping paths where feelings sway.
Together we weave, hand in hand,
A lattice of longing, forever planned.

Colorations of Courage

In hues of red, hearts beat strong,
A palette where the brave belong.
With every shade, a story told,
Of battles fought and of the bold.

Through storms of doubt, they paint the sky,
In strokes of gold, they will not shy.
Vibrant greens of hope arise,
In the canvas where courage lies.

With splashes bright, they light the night,
Their colors clash, yet feel so right.
From darkest blues to radiant white,
Courage blooms, a beautiful sight.

Each color blends, a song of grace,
In every heart, a sacred space.
Together they stand, strong and free,
In the art of bravery, we see.

Singular Patterns

Amid the chaos, a thread holds tight,
In patterns woven, a guiding light.
Each twist and turn, a dance of fate,
Unique in rhythm, never late.

The line of life draws paths anew,
A singular journey, just for you.
In echoes soft, sweet whispers call,
Patterns emerge, embracing all.

Through tangled vines, a beauty grows,
In every leaf, the story flows.
Singular paths that intertwine,
In hearts of many, one design.

From fractal stems to endless skies,
In every glance, the wonder lies.
Embrace the strange, the dreamer's art,
In singular patterns, we find our heart.

The Architecture of Awakening

In dawn's soft light, the world takes shape,
Brick by brick, a new escape.
Foundations built on deep resolve,
In waking dreams, we start to evolve.

Arches curve, reaching for the sun,
With every step, the race begun.
Windows open to endless skies,
In this structure, hope never lies.

The blueprint raw, yet pure of heart,
In every flaw, a work of art.
Creating spaces, we come alive,
In the architecture, we thrive.

As shadows dance on ancient walls,
Awakening whispers, as the light calls.
In every heartbeat, the vision's near,
A beautiful home, once cloaked in fear.

Landscapes of Lullabies

In fields of peace, the soft winds sigh,
Nature sings as stars draw nigh.
Gentle streams hum a soothing tune,
In twilight's glow, beneath the moon.

Mountains cradle dreams so high,
Their silence whispers, never lie.
Every valley holds a song,
In the quiet where hearts belong.

Breezes flow through canopies wide,
In dappled shade, sweet dreams abide.
The fragrance of night blooms sweetly here,
A symphony that calms all fear.

In lullabies that nature weaves,
We find the rest that each heart needs.
A landscape painted in shadows and light,
In tranquil spaces, all feels right.

The Frameworks of Serendipity

In shadows where the whispers grow,
Chance encounters softly flow.
Paths entwine in secret ways,
Guiding hearts through sunlit days.

Each moment holds a hidden door,
A dance of fate, forevermore.
Unseen threads that softly weave,
Dreams unfold, and we believe.

With every twist and every turn,
Life's sweet lessons we can learn.
Amidst the chaos and the noise,
Serendipity brings us joys.

In laughter shared and glances bright,
Finding magic in the night.
Embrace the gifts the day will send,
As all our stories intertwine, transcend.

In the Wake of Night's Dreams

Softly call the twilight's grace,
Stars awaken in their place.
In the stillness, spirits roam,
Guiding wanderers back home.

Echoes of the day now fade,
In shadows, new paths are laid.
Whispers linger, sweet and low,
In dreams, we find where we must go.

The sea of night, a canvas wide,
Where hopes and fears in silence bide.
With every breath, the visions pour,
Unlocking worlds we can explore.

As moonbeams dance on fabric rare,
The heart will soar, the mind will dare.
In the dreamscape, we ignite,
Embracing dawn's soft, golden light.

Architects of Ambition

In the heart, a vision stirs,
Driven by the dreams it purrs.
Blueprints crafted, step by step,
Building bridges where we've leapt.

Chasing shadows, forging light,
Every challenge takes its flight.
Structures rise from steadfast will,
As we climb the daunting hill.

With hands that shape both future and past,
In the forge of dreams, we hold steadfast.
Every doubt a brick laid down,
A castle built that wears a crown.

Together we will trace the lines,
In harmony, ambition shines.
With vision clear, we will defend,
As architects, we rise, transcend.

Schematics of Stardust

Across the vast celestial stream,
We sketch the night, we weave the dream.
Every star, a tale unknown,
A universe where seeds are sown.

In cosmic gardens, dreams take flight,
Clustered close in soft, twilight.
We are but stardust, so divine,
Mapping out the grand design.

With fingers painted in the light,
Tracing fates through endless night.
Schematics drawn in whispers true,
Calling us to start anew.

In every spark, a promise bright,
To guide us through the endless night.
Together, we will chart our course,
With stardust dreams, we find our force.

Etiquette of Envisioning

In silence, dreams take flight,
Whispers of the soul arise.
With soft intent, we create,
Visions painted in the skies.

With every thought, a seed sown,
Cultivating a world anew.
Breathe in hope, let shadows fade,
In the garden, let love bloom.

Mind the paths where spirits walk,
Guiding light through doubt and fear.
Gentle hands shape the contours,
Crafting futures with our tear.

Time flows gently, moments pause,
Every heartbeat, a chance to see.
Envision a space where all belong,
A tapestry of harmony.

Fibonacci of Wishes

Each wish unfolds, a spiral dance,
Layers deep, like nature's code.
In sequences, we find our way,
A symphony of hearts bestowed.

First, a spark, then dreams expand,
Echoes of hope in soft refrain.
In this pattern, we connect,
An infinite loop of joy and pain.

From twinkling stars to oceans wide,
The Fibonacci sings its song.
Wishes blooming in perfect time,
Together we rise, forever strong.

Count the ways we twine our fates,
In numbers, love will softly thread.
With every layer, we discover,
The beauty in what lies ahead.

Constructs of the Heart

Brick by brick, we build our dreams,
Foundations laid with sweat and tears.
Each fragment tells of hope and grace,
A sanctuary from our fears.

Walls adorned with laughter's echo,
Windows to the soul's embrace.
Each room a story waiting still,
In the constructs, we find our place.

An arch of trust, a door of care,
In every corner, love will dwell.
From vision's spark to life's design,
In this home, our hearts will swell.

Together we'll face the storms of life,
With strong foundations, hand in hand.
In the heart's blueprints, we find strength,
As love will guide us through this land.

Journeys in Ink

With pen in hand, adventures call,
Through paper realms, we dare to roam.
Each word a path, both wide and small,
In every line, we find our home.

Ink spills stories, rich and bright,
Winding streets of courage and fear.
Characters dance in the soft moonlight,
In fleeting moments, truth is clear.

Chasing horizons, searching deep,
Through scribbles, we unravel fate.
In the margins, secrets sleep,
Each page a chance to create.

A journey penned beneath the stars,
In every chapter, dreams ignite.
Through journeys in ink, we chart our way,
Finding solace in the night.

The Symphony of the Soul

In whispers soft, the shadows play,
A dance of light, the night's ballet.
Melodies float in twilight's hue,
Each note a secret, fresh and new.

Where hopes collide with dreams untold,
The heartbeats echo, fierce and bold.
Together they weave a tapestry,
Of love and loss, eternity.

In every sigh, there's music sweet,
A harmony where souls do meet.
The symphony swells, wild and free,
An endless song, just you and me.

Through every storm, through every tear,
The chorus rises, strong and clear.
In stillness found, our spirits soar,
The symphony plays forevermore.

Design by Day

The sun ascends, a canvas bright,
Brushes of gold, the morning light.
New sketches drawn in azure skies,
Nature's palette, a sweet surprise.

Each petal blooms, a tale to tell,
In gardens where the dreamers dwell.
With every dawn, fresh visions grow,
A world reborn, aglow in flow.

The winds of change, they stir the leaves,
In whispered notes, the heart believes.
Every moment, a chance to start,
A design crafted from the heart.

As hours pass, the shadows blend,
The day's creation finds its end.
With twilight's kiss, our dreams entwine,
A masterpiece, divine, benign.

The Art of Elysium

In fields where golden poppies sway,
A blissful breath, a soft ballet.
Where stars are born in silent night,
And dreams take wing for skies in flight.

With every heartbeat, peace resides,
In gentle waves, where love abides.
The world, a canvas painted bright,
In hues of love and pure delight.

Each moment, sacred, soft and true,
Awakens all that's lost to view.
With laughter ringing in the air,
We find our place, beyond all care.

In Elysium's embrace we share,
A fleeting glance, a sacred prayer.
The art of life, in balance, glows,
A timeless dance, where beauty flows.

Mutable Visions

The mind, a river, swift and wide,
Dreams drift and swirl, like ocean tide.
Thoughts dance in colors, bright and bold,
Stories unfold, like threads of gold.

With every turn, our paths may shift,
In shadows cast, our spirits lift.
A canvas stretched, forever new,
Mutable visions, shifting view.

In fleeting moments, truth revealed,
In whispered hopes, the heart is healed.
With visions boundless, we will roam,
A quest for light, a search for home.

So let us wander, hold our dreams,
In changing tides, where nothing seems.
For every moment bears its gift,
In mutable visions, our souls uplift.

Echoes of Tomorrow

In the dawn's soft light, we stand anew,
Dreams dance lightly, weaving through.
Footprints of hope on the silken ground,
Echoes of tomorrow, a sweet, soft sound.

Waves of the future call us near,
With whispers of joy, they soothe our fear.
Each step a promise, each breath a chance,
In the melody of life, we find our stance.

Stars above twinkle, guiding the way,
Illuminating paths where shadows play.
With hearts wide open, we chase the sun,
In echoes of tomorrow, we find our fun.

As twilight falls, we gather dreams,
In the quiet moments, hope brightly gleams.
Together we forge, with passion we strive,
In the echoes of tomorrow, we come alive.

Whispers in the Fabric

Threads of the past weave through the now,
In whispers of fabric, we take a bow.
Every stitch a memory, a tale to share,
In the loom of life, we find our care.

Colors blend softly, as time unfolds,
Tales of the heart in the stories told.
Glimmers of laughter and tears we sew,
In whispers of fabric, our truths will show.

Patterns emerge from the chaos we know,
A tapestry woven from joy and woe.
With every heartbeat, a new thread spins,
In the whispers of fabric, our journey begins.

As night drapes softly, we wrap in dreams,
In the warmth of the fabric, hope always beams.
Together we stitch the future so bright,
In whispers of fabric, we find the light.

The Architecture of Ambitions

Blueprints of dreams, sketched in time,
Foundations of vision, bold and sublime.
Each brick laid carefully, a step we take,
The architecture of ambitions, we create.

Windows of promise, open wide,
Letting in sunlight, our hearts inside.
Roofs of resilience shelter our fight,
In the architecture of ambitions, we ignite.

Hallways of hope stretch into the sky,
With every heartbeat, we reach up high.
Staircases spiral, paths intertwine,
In the architecture of ambitions, we shine.

As seasons change, our plans evolve,
In the blueprint of life, problems dissolve.
Together we build, with passion and dreams,
In the architecture of ambitions, we are beams.

Sketches of a Stardust Journey

On the canvas of night, we paint with stars,
Sketches of a journey, near and far.
With brushes of moonlight, we trace the way,
In the stardust of dreams, we choose to sway.

Galaxies whisper secrets untold,
In every twinkle, a treasure to hold.
Our hearts as compasses, this path we roam,
In sketches of stardust, we find our home.

Constellations guide through shadows and light,
In the tapestry woven of day and night.
With wings of ambition, we soar and glide,
In the sketches of a stardust journey, we bide.

As we wander through time, with spirits so free,
A dance of the cosmos, in harmony.
In the sketches of stardust, our stories blend,
With love as our anchor, on hopes we depend.

The Skeleton of Unseen Futures

In shadows deep, they linger still,
Whispers of paths we dare not chase.
Ghosts of dreams that time won't kill,
Forming shapes without a face.

Threads of fate in darkened skies,
Cast their nets on silent shores.
Each heartbeat sings its soft goodbyes,
While the unknown softly roars.

Among the echoes, shadows play,
Future's breath is cold yet bright.
We tread on timid hopes each day,
Yearning for a glimpse of light.

In twilight's grasp, we find our song,
A harmony of lost and found.
In the dusk where dreams belong,
Futures dance on haunted ground.

Foundations of a Wish

Beneath the stars, a seed is sown,
A tender thought, a silent vow.
In quiet hearts, foundations grown,
The weight of hope we choose to allow.

With whispered winds, they flutter near,
Fragile dreams take root in night.
Each wish we nurture, bright and clear,
Transforms the dark to radiant light.

In gardens deep, our thoughts will bloom,
Petals soft, with colors rare.
Rising high to chase the gloom,
Carried forth by gentle air.

Building skies with every prayer,
A future forged in gleaming rays.
Foundations strong, in love and care,
We'll shape the world in endless ways.

Mosaics of Light and Shadow

In every crack, the colors dance,
Fragments shining in the gloom.
Mosaics shaped by chance and chance,
Creating beauty out of doom.

Whispers of the past remain,
In patterns woven, stories told.
Light mixes well with hints of pain,
In every piece, a heart of gold.

Shard by shard, the picture grows,
Reflecting tales of joy and woe.
In the play of light, love shows,
Each shadow deepens what we know.

Collecting fragments, we will find,
In chaos lies a brilliant art.
Mosaics of both heart and mind,
Are stitched together, never part.

Dream Weavings in Paper Seas

On paper tides, our thoughts take flight,
Crafted dreams on waves of fate.
Sailing forth into the night,
Weaving stories we create.

In ink and whispers, worlds unfold,
Boundless seas of hope and mirth.
Every tale a thread of gold,
Sewn together with the earth.

In creased maps where visions lay,
Journeys start with whispered sighs.
Beyond the shores, we drift, we sway,
Chasing echoes, endless skies.

With every stroke, the dreams take form,
In distant realms where wishes play.
We sail through calm and raging storm,
Searching for the light of day.

Navigating the Ethereal Fields

In fields where whispers weave the sky,
Stars murmur secrets as they fly.
The moonlight dances on silver streams,
Guiding wanderers through starlit dreams.

Gentle breezes carry soft delight,
As shadows blend into the night.
Each step taken, a story unfolds,
In ethereal realms where magic holds.

With every heartbeat, the soul takes flight,
Lost in the beauty, embracing the night.
Navigating paths where spirits roam,
Finding solace in the vast unknown.

A journey woven in threads of grace,
In the quiet, we find our place.
Through ethereal fields, we are set free,
Embracing the whispers of eternity.

Portraits of Tomorrow's Light

Each brushstroke paints a vivid dream,
Future's canvas in colors that gleam.
Visions of hope in every hue,
A portrait of what could be, anew.

Beneath the sun's warm, radiant glow,
Ideas blossom, steadily grow.
Artists carve paths, uncharted ways,
Illuminating hearts with brighter days.

Brush in hand, they shape the dawn,
With every stroke, a new world drawn.
Tomorrow's light, a promise so bright,
In portraits of dreams, we find our flight.

From shadows of doubt, we rise above,
Crafting a future, guided by love.
In vivid colors, our stories blend,
Each portrait a vision that will transcend.

The Artistry of Ambition's Forge

In fires of passion, dreams ignite,
Ambition's forge, where spirits unite.
Crafting visions from molten fate,
Chasing horizons, we create.

With hammer strikes, the future forms,
Against the odds, we weather storms.
Each spark a step on paths we tread,
In artistry, our dreams are fed.

Through trials faced, the spirit grows,
In sculpted hope, the journey shows.
Forging destinies with grit and grace,
The artistry of time we embrace.

From ashes rise, renewed and bold,
In the forge of life, our stories told.
Ambition's fire, a guiding star,
Illuminates the wonders near and far.

Beneath the Arch of a Wish

Under the arch where wishes soar,
Dreams take flight to an open door.
Each hope a lantern, glowing bright,
Illuminating the depths of night.

With whispered prayers, we seek and find,
The magic woven within the mind.
Beneath the stars, intentions blend,
In the silent moments, souls transcend.

A tapestry spun with threads of grace,
In the arch's embrace, we find our place.
Wishes uplifted on wings of light,
Guiding us home through shadowed night.

In the stillness, echoes of dreams,
Beneath the arch, life's promise gleams.
With every wish cast into the air,
We paint our hopes, a canvas rare.

Synergy of Vision

Together we rise, hand in hand,
With dreams that merge, a common strand.
In whispered thoughts, our hearts align,
A tapestry bright, your soul and mine.

Through stormy seas, we find our way,
Navigating light in shades of gray.
Each step we take, in harmony,
Crafts a future, bold and free.

In unity's bond, we stand as one,
A melody played, not yet begun.
With each vision shared, we touch the sky,
In the dance of life, together we fly.

Let the world see our radiant spark,
Igniting hope, igniting the dark.
In synergy's embrace, we find the call,
With visions entwined, we rise, we fall.

The Well of Yearning

In the depths of silence, echoes fade,
Where dreams once lingered, hopes displayed.
A whisper calls from the shadowed deep,
In the quiet corners, secrets seep.

With every wish upon a star,
We trace the path of who we are.
Searching for solace in the night,
Beneath the veil, the heart takes flight.

The well of yearning, deep and wide,
Carries our hopes with the ebbing tide.
Each drop of longing, a story told,
In its embrace, both warm and cold.

Let the waters cleanse the weary soul,
Find strength in the search, regain control.
In the depths of yearning, we may see,
The promise of what we long to be.

Refinements of Resolve

In the forge of trials, we are made,
Each challenge faced, our fears displayed.
With every stumble, we rise anew,
Refined by fire, our spirits grew.

Through valleys low and peaks that call,
We stand unwavering, refusing to fall.
Our resolve as strong as iron laid,
With each new dawn, our strength remade.

In the dance of struggle, we find grace,
Embracing change, we carve our space.
With lessons learned, we craft our fate,
A tapestry woven, never too late.

Refinements true, in hardship found,
Hidden treasures in the battleground.
In the journey's end, we stand fulfilled,
With hearts alive, our dreams instilled.

Gardens of Hope

In gardens lush, where wildflowers bloom,
A tapestry woven dispels the gloom.
Each seed a promise, a love unspoken,
In gentle whispers, our hearts are broken.

Tender shoots rise, reaching for light,
In their pursuit, we find our might.
With every color, a story shared,
In the soil of dreams, love is bared.

Through seasons changing, we patiently wait,
Cultivating faith, nurturing fate.
In the warmth of sun, and rain's soft kiss,
We find the essence of purest bliss.

Gardens of hope, where sorrows untwine,
Creating a space where hearts align.
In every bloom, a chance to revive,
In this sacred haven, we come alive.

Chronicles of Creation

In the beginning, light unveiled,
Stars ignited, dreams enthralled,
Whispers of worlds, softly breathed,
Endless stories, yet untold.

Waters rose, and mountains grew,
Fires danced in the evening hue,
Nature's canvas, vast and wide,
Every creature found its stride.

Time spun on, a rhythmic tide,
Life emerged, no place to hide,
Joy and sorrow, hand in hand,
Crafting paths across the land.

With each dawn, new tales unfold,
In the heart, a spark of gold,
Chronicles lost, but now we've found,
In creation's grip, we're bound.

Inked Inspirations

With pen in hand, I chart my fight,
On pages bare, I seek the light,
Words like rivers, flow and twist,
In ink, my dreams persist.

Stories whispered in every line,
Woven thoughts like sacred vine,
In shadows dark, my hope ignites,
Inked inspirations, take to flight.

Each chapter a dance, a vibrant hue,
Reflections of hearts, both old and new,
Casting visions in the air,
In every breath, art lays bare.

Through storms of doubt, I boldly tread,
My soul bared for all to read,
Inked inspirations, brave and true,
In every word, my spirit grew.

Dimensions of Delight

In every corner, joy resides,
A bloom that on the heart abides,
Each smile shared, a spark so bright,
In dimensions framed by pure delight.

From twilight's glow to dawn's embrace,
Every moment, a treasured space,
Laughter echoes, sweet and clear,
In this world, love conquers fear.

Colors dance in skies of blue,
Nature's palette, rich and true,
In quiet stillness, bliss is found,
In each heartbeat's gentle sound.

Crafting memories in the day,
Dimensions shift in every way,
With open hearts, we live the best,
In dimensions of delight, we rest.

Echoes in the Ether

In the vastness, whispers soar,
Echoes linger, forever more,
Thoughts and dreams collide in flight,
Carried softly through the night.

Voices of time, a distant song,
In the ether, they belong,
Moments captured, truths revealed,
In echoes, hearts are healed.

Each breath a note, a symphony,
Waves of wonder, wild and free,
In shadows cast by light's embrace,
Echoes dance in boundless space.

Together we weave, a cosmic thread,
In the ether, where dreams are led,
An endless journey, pure and bright,
Echoes guide us through the night.

Milton Keynes UK
Ingram Content Group UK Ltd.
UKHW032036191024
449814UK00010B/470

9 789916 880470